The Little Book Of
Chords For Guitar

3.99

Exclusive distributors:
Music Sales Limited
14 15 Berners Street, London W1T 3LJ, England.
Music Sales Pty Limited
Units 3-4, 17 Willfox St,
Condell Park, NSW 2200 Australia.

Order No.AM954778
ISBN 0-7119-7822-0
This book © Copyright 1999 by Wise Publications

Written by Rikky Rooksby
Book engraved and designed by Digital Music Art
Photographs by George Taylor

Cover design by Trickett & Webb

Printed in the United Kingdom

Your Guarantee of Quality
As publishers, we strive to produce every book to the highest commercial
standards. Particular care has been given to specifying acid-free, neutral-sized paper
made from pulps which have not been elemental chlorine bleached. This pulp is from
farmed sustainable forests and was produced with special regard for the environment.
Throughout, the printing and binding have been planned to ensure a sturdy,
attractive publication which should give years of enjoyment.
If your copy fails to meet our high standards, please inform us and we will gladly replace it.

www.musicsales.com

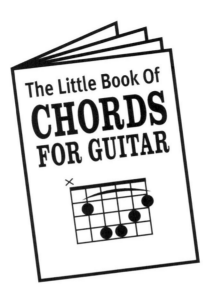

The Little Book Of
CHORDS
FOR GUITAR

Wise Publications
London/New York/Sydney/Paris/Copenhagen/Madrid

Contents

Introduction

Music has three basic elements: melody, harmony and rhythm. All popular songs comprise these three elements - you hear a tune (melody), a beat, (rhythm), and chords, (harmony). Harmony - or using chords under a melody line - is important because it adds interest and 'colour' to the music.

In this Little Book of Chords, you'll learn how to build and extend your chord knowledge substantially, and find out how to use the right chords to play all your favourite songs!

Chord Diagrams Explained

Fretboxes show the guitar upright *i.e.* with the headstock, nut and tuning pegs at the top of the picture – six vertical lines represent the strings.

The x symbol means you should not play this string

The o symbol means play the string 'open' without fretting a note

The thick black line represents the nut of the guitar

Numbers in a circle show which finger you should use to fret the note. Numbers shown in black are the 'root' of the chord – *ie* its letter name

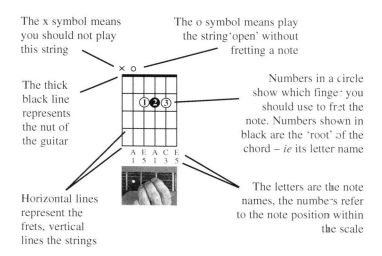

Horizontal lines represent the frets, vertical lines the strings

The letters are the note names, the numbers refer to the note position within the scale

What makes a chord? Have a look at the first three chord boxes. In the first there's a single note C; in the second the E and G above that note have been added. Those three notes C E G make the chord of C major.

With just three notes it is harmonically complete - however, when playing a guitar we want to generate more sound. In the third chord box we have added another C and E, instantly creating a much bigger sound.

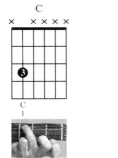

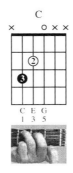

In these next three boxes, the same process can be seen creating a G major chord.

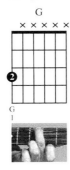

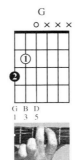

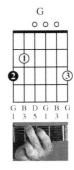

What Is A Triad?

A triad is simply a chord made up of 3 notes. Many chords have 3 notes in them; however, on the guitar, some of these can be repeated in other places on the fretboard. A triad has only 3 notes in it, and in order for us to know what chord it is, it must include the root, third and fifth notes of the scale. See the four triads below; they all include C as the root note, which indicates a 'C' chord.

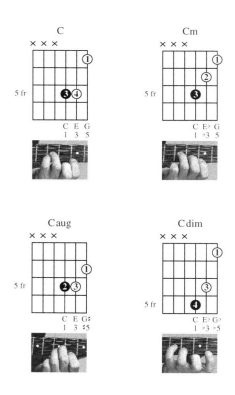

The Four Triad Types

In making a triad the distance between the 1st and middle note, and between the middle and top note, must be a major or minor third. A major third is two tones (4 frets) and a minor third is one and a half tones (3 frets). The four triad types are the four possible combinations of these intervals and three notes:

How to calculate triads

Chord	Interval and distance from previous chord tone (in tones)				
Box 1 (C)	Root	3rd	2	5th	1 1/2
Box 2 (Cm)	Root	♭3rd	1 1/2	5th	2
Box 3 (Caug)	Root	3rd	2	♯5th	2
Box 4 (Cdim)	Root	♭3rd	1 1/2	♭5th	1 1/2

Notice the difference in the sound of the triads - the minor sounds sad in comparison to the major. Major and minor chords are used in most songs, while the diminished and augmented triads are quite rare because of their awkward sound.

C, C everywhere

Although triads by themselves don't make enough sound to be a good accompaniment, they can be useful in other musical situations. As a triad only uses three notes, it can be found in many different places on the fretboard.

These next eight boxes show a variety of C major triads at different pitches and places on the neck.

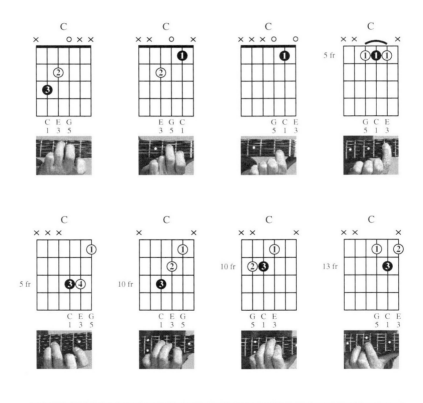

The next set of chord boxes give shapes for the major and minor triads on each combination of adjacent strings. Notice that the triads on strings 1-2-3 and 2-3-4 have a clearer sound than those on 3-4-5 and 4-5-6. Triads tend to sound 'muddy' when played on the lower strings - consequently, these lower triads sound better if the notes are picked one after the other. This gives the ear a chance to differentiate between the notes.

The triad shapes on the top strings are found not only in rhythm playing but also in lead guitar, where they function as an alternative to using scales.

If you find any of the fingerings slightly awkward, use a first finger barre where appropriate.

The shapes are given in a set sequence in which the root note is first the lowest of the three, then in the middle, then at the top of the shape. Specific note names are not given on these triads because they are designed to be moveable. All you need to remember is where the root note is out of the three strings.

Another point to notice about the shapes is that on strings 3-4-5 and 4-5-6 the shape remains the same; it just moves one string lower. This happens because the interval between these strings is always a fourth.

Major Triad Shapes

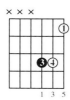

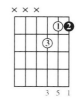

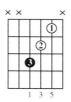

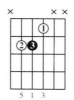

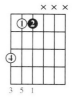

1 ♭3 5

5 1 ♭3

♭3 5 1

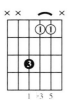

1 ♭3 5

5 1 ♭3

♭3 5 1

1 ♭3 5

5 1 ♭3

♭3 5 1

1 ♭3 5

5 1 ♭3

♭3 5 1

Major Chords

Let's have a look at some of the most common chords used in popular music, whether it's folk, pop, rock, blues or soul. Here are the shapes for A, B, C, D, E, F and G majors. B and F can be difficult at first, so initially try the simplified shapes shown.

The boxes tell you where to put your fingers, how many strings are fretted or open, which notes you're playing and which position of the scale each note is.

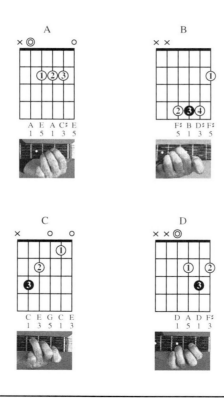

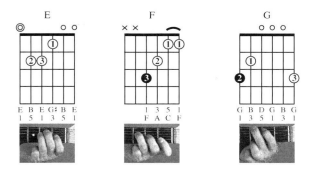

Moveable Shapes

The three extra boxes (B, F and C♯/D♭) are moveable shapes, *ie:* they can be moved up and down the neck to get the sharp/flat chords (A♯/B♭, C♯/D♭, D♯/E♭, F♯/G♭, G♯/A♭). Use the lowest 'root' note (coloured black on the boxes) to locate the desired chord. As long as you keep the rest of the shape the same it will sound correct wherever you move it on the neck.

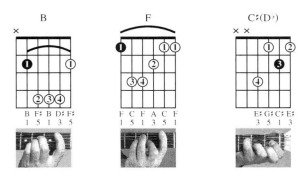

Sharp / Flat Major Chords

Here are the most common ways of playing the sharp/flat major chords. Experiment with fingering to find the easiest shapes for you.

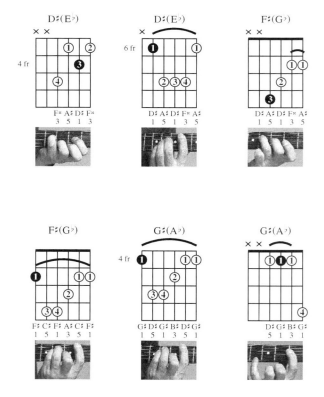

If you find the second A♯/B♭ with the barre too hard at first, play the first version for this chord. The third box is a variant fingering popular with electric players - it sacrifices the top note of the chord but removes the need for a barre.

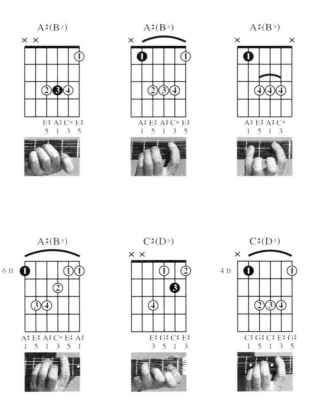

Five G Chords

Sometimes small variations on a shape are possible, which you can often see in books of sheet music. Here are five G major chords, each with a slightly different sound to the others. Choose the best one for the particular sound you want, or if it fits into your chord sequence better.

The G in the third box, for example, leaves the first and second fingers free to add notes and then take them away (as happens in Sheryl Crow's 'If It Makes You Happy' and David Bowie's 'John I'm Only Dancing'). The version in box 2 is a Noel Gallagher favourite.

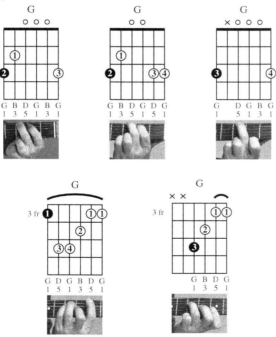

Here are the chord shapes for the minor chords. Bm, Cm, Fm and Gm can be difficult at first, so initially try these abbreviated forms. You'll notice that the root notes for Bm and Cm are not at the bottom of the chord - these are called 'slash' chords - but we'll come to them later.

The two extra boxes (Bm, Fm) are moveable shapes and can be moved up or down the neck to get the sharp/flat minor chords. Use the lowest 'root' note (numbered 1, in black, on the boxes) to locate the desired chord as before.

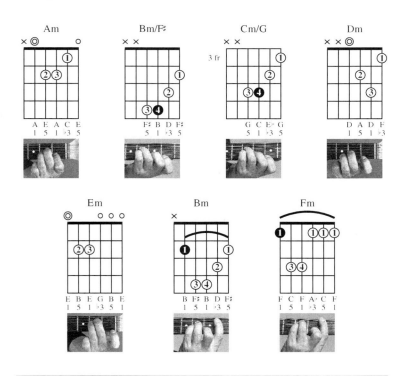

Six Minor Chords

Any chord on the guitar can be played in a number of places. The rule is: the simpler the chord, the greater the number of positions. Here are six different A minors.

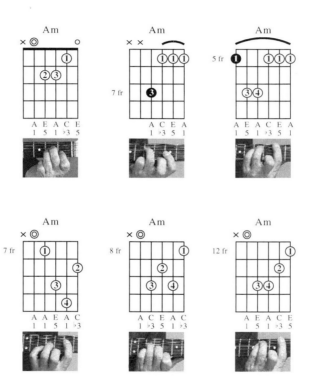

Here are the most common ways of playing the sharp/flat minor chords. If you find the second A♯m/B♭m with the barre too hard at first, play the first shape for this chord. With box 3 - C♯m - be very careful not to hit the fifth string as it will instantly turn this into a major 7th chord!

Although F♯m and G♯m can be played with the shape shown in box 2, they would have to be quite high up the neck, so it is uncommon to play these chords anywhere other than at frets II and IV.

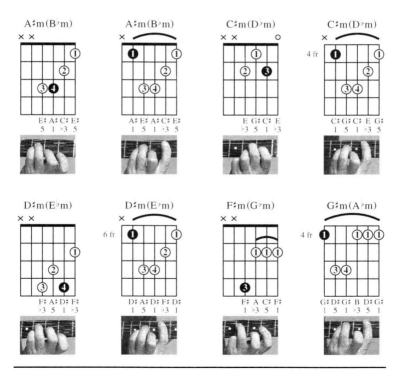

21

Slash Chords: First Inversion Major

There are many different types of chord, and in Part Three we'll be exploring the most popular, which are created by adding one or two extra notes to the three which make up a simple major or minor chord. But before we do that, there are two other types of chord to look at which don't involve adding any notes to what we already have.

They are called 'inversions' and are created by changing the lowest note in the chord. In a simple major or minor chord there are three notes - in C major, C E G. If C is at the bottom we have a root position chord - but if we put the middle note (known as the third) at the bottom (here an E) we have what is called a 'first inversion' chord.

Compared to the root chord, a first inversion has a mobile quality - it sounds like it wants to move somewhere. The bass note wants to either rise or fall a step. For this reason the most frequent use of first inversion chords is in descending chord progressions, linking the bass notes, such as this:

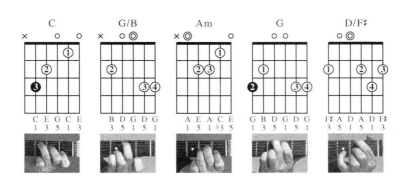

Here are eight common first inversion chords - notated with a slash - hence the name 'slash chord'. The first letter name is the chord name, the second refers to the bass note. E.g: C/E simply means that it's a chord of C with E - the third - at the bottom. You'll notice that the root note (in black) is no longer the lowest note of the chord.

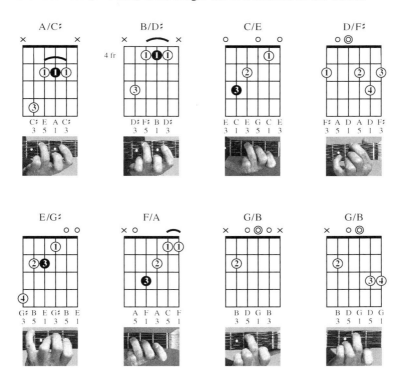

If you play in a band and you want to explore inversions, just get your bass player to change his note. That's an easier way of doing it.

Second Inversion Major

Second inversion chords are the other option for changing the basic sound of a major or minor chord.

It's important to refer to the triad when trying to build second inversion chords. If you always think of the chord as three notes - root, third and fifth, it's easy to find the bass note for a second inversion chord - always use the fifth. For example, if the chord of C major consists of the notes C (root), E (third) and G (fifth), then by putting G at the bottom of the chord, you have created a second inversion!

Here's the chord C/G.

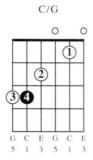

Notice that it is almost exactly the same as a standard C major chord, except with the addition of the third finger on the bottom string, creating the note of G.

The general point to remember about inversions is that a few inversions inserted between root chords can make for more interesting music, especially on softer, ballad-type material. You can hear second and first inversion chords on the intro to Jimi Hendrix's famous 'The Wind Cries Mary'.

Here are six more second inversion major chords. You will notice that they don't sound as mobile as first inversion chords. Play these and listen to the difference.

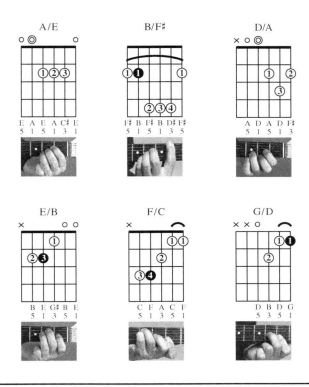

First Inversion Minor

It's also possible to invert minor chords. If C minor is C E♭ G, we can turn it into a first inversion chord by using E♭ as the lowest note. First inversion minor chords have the effect of slightly intensifying the sad quality of the minor chord. This is because the note that makes the chord minor, the 'flattened third', is at the bottom.

Here are six first inversion minor chords.

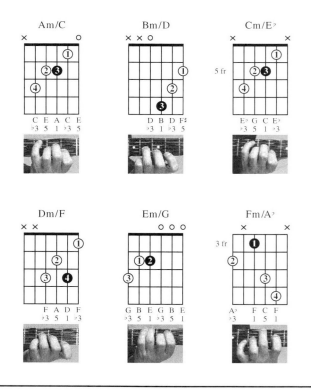

There are also second inversion minor chords, but they're not used often, as a chord progression with only second inversion minor chords would sound even dreamier than a second inversion major progression. Here are some chord shapes.

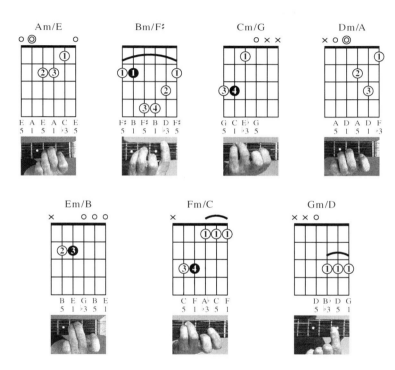

The golden rule of inversions is: the number of possible inversions is always one less than the number of notes in a chord.

Power-Chords / Fifth Chords

You may have heard or read of 'power chords' and wondered what they were. The proper name for a power-chord is a 'fifth' and they are written C^5, E^5 etc. Here's why...

If we compare a C major triad (C E G) with a C minor triad (C E♭ G) it is clear that the only difference between them is the note in the middle, the 'third'. If we remove this, we are left with C and G, which are an interval of a fifth apart, and therefore create a 'power-chord'. The removal of the third also means that the power-chord is neutral - neither major nor minor.

The fifth (or power-chord) has a powerful, gritty sound making it central to rock music - usually played at high volume and with maximum distortion!

Check out these next chord boxes for some examples of power-chords. Notice the last chord box - instead of the root note being at the bottom, it uses the fifth, which gives it a sort of 'second inversion' quality.

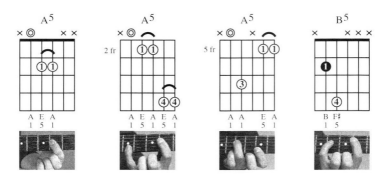

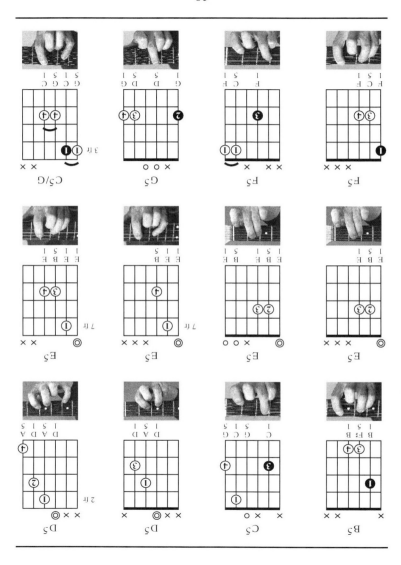

Chord Voicing

Let's have another look at some of the open major and minor chords. One of the guitar's great features is that the tonal contrasts between the same type of chord is much greater than on an instrument like the piano. This is because of the mixture of fretted with open strings and the way that mixture interacts with the presence of different combinations of roots, thirds and fifths within a chord. The table on page 31 should give you some idea of how many different combinations there are.

For each chord the table shows which strings are played, whether they are open or fretted, and which degree of the scale they represent (root, third or fifth).

Whether it's the combination of fretted against open strings, how many strings are played, or how many roots, thirds or fifths are involved, the table shows the great variety of sound which exists even among chords of the same type. With experience it is possible to tune your ears to recognise these differences, with the result that you will find it possible to hear what chords are being used in a song, and even what key it is in.

To use a visual analogy, if hearing the difference between a major chord and a minor is like seeing blue or red, then hearing the difference in these chord voicings is like distinguishing between different tones, or shades, of those colours.

Chord Voicing Table

String Number

	6	5	4	3	2	1
A major	x	open	fretted	fretted	fretted	open
	x	1	5	1	3	5
C major	x	fretted	fretted	open	fretted	open
	x	1	3	5	3	5
D major	x	x	open	fretted	fretted	fretted
	x	x	1	5	1	3
E major	open	fretted	fretted	fretted	open	open
	1	5	1	3	5	1
G major	fretted	fretted	open	open	open	fretted
	1	3	5	1	3	1
A minor	x	open	fretted	fretted	fretted	open
	x	1	5	1	♭3	5
D minor	x	x	open	fretted	fretted	fretted
	x	x	1	5	1	♭3
E minor	open	fretted	fretted	open	open	open
	1	5	1	♭3	5	1

Dominant Seventh

After majors and minors, one of the next most popular chords is the dominant seventh. This is formed by adding the note which is one tone below the root note. **C7 = C E G B♭**.

Here are ten examples of dominant sevenths. When adding a note to a basic chord, remember that it sounds more effective if it is higher up than the other notes. For example, listen to the difference between the sound of the first and second A7's.

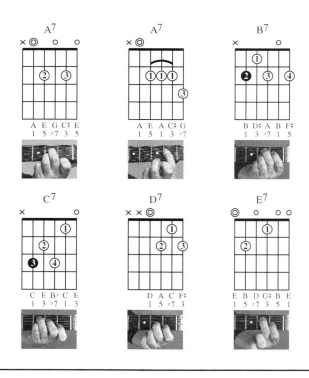

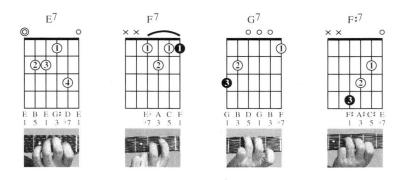

Moveable shapes

Use these three extra boxes as moveable shapes to find any other dominant seventh you need.

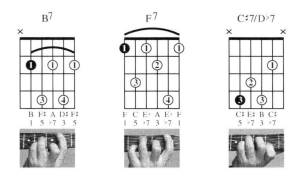

The dominant seventh is often used to reinforce a sense of key, to change key, and will 'toughen-up' a chord sequence. It is used heavily in blues and rock.

Major Seventh

Another popular chord is the major seventh. This is formed by adding the note which is one semitone below the root. **Cmaj⁷ = C E G B.**

Here are eight major sevenths. Notice the contrast in sound between the two Amaj⁷'s and the two Emaj⁷'s. Again, this is due to the placement of the seventh note within the chord; the higher up, the more prominent it is.

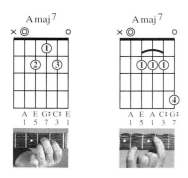

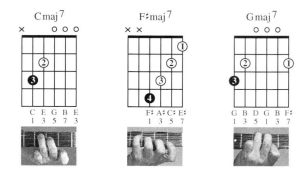

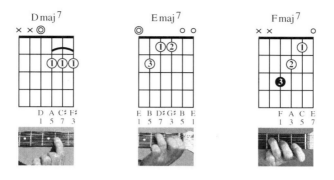

Moveable Shapes

Use the Bmaj^7 and second Emaj^7 moveable shapes to find any major seventh you need.

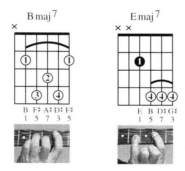

Like the dominant seventh, the major seventh is also a major chord, but it has a very different tone. It is a gentle, romantic chord, capable of evoking many reflective and tender emotions. For this reason it is not used much in blues or rock but is vital for ballads, MOR and soul music. The major seventh will 'soften' a chord sequence, and works better at medium to slow tempos.

Minor Seventh

Minor chords can also become sevenths. The minor seventh is formed by adding the note which is one tone below the root of a minor chord. **Cm^7 = C E$\flat$ G B$\flat$.**

Here are ten minor seventh chords. Notice the contrast in sound between the two Am^7 and the two Em^7 chords. In the latter case the second Em^7 chord has a stronger minor sound.

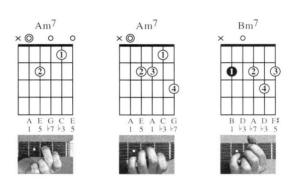

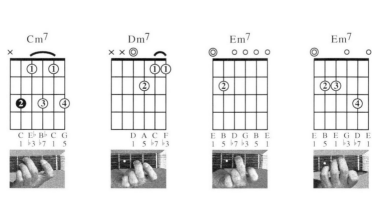

The minor seventh is a diluted form of the straight minor. If a song progression sounds too sad with minor chords, try replacing some of them with their minor seventh forms. The minor seventh is a very adaptable chord, and occurs in songs from most music genres, from folk-songs to the hard rock of Thin Lizzy's classic 'The Boys Are Back In Town' and The Beatles' 'I Want You'.

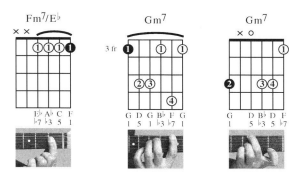

Moveable Shapes

Use the Bm⁷ and the Fm⁷ moveable shapes to find any other minor seventh you need.

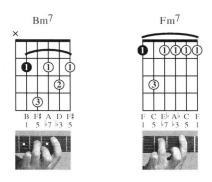

The Minor (Major) Seventh

Here's an exotic type of minor seventh. The minor (major) seventh is formed by adding the note which is a semitone below the root of a minor chord. $Cm^{maj7} = C$ E♭ G B. Here are eight minor (major) sevenths.

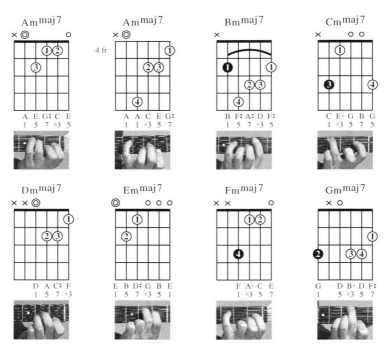

The minor (major) 7 is a tense, atmospheric chord almost never used on its own for more than a bar. It's used as a passing chord, linking a minor with an ordinary minor seventh. Its ability to create a spooky atmosphere makes it popular with soundtrack composers - its most well-known use being for the classic 60's James Bond films - hence my nickname for it: the '00minor7'.

Diminished Seventh

The diminished seventh is a chord built on the diminished triad, entirely made up of minor third intervals - 1½ tones away from each other.

Extremely rare in rock or pop, this chord is used mostly in jazz, partly because it enables the music to change key and is usually found as a passing chord. It would produce a strange, unsettling sound if held for longer than a couple of beats.

One of its strangest features is that any of the four notes can be regarded as the root note. As a result you will notice that each of these chord boxes has five or six names!

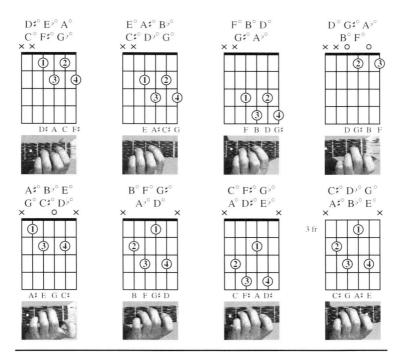

39

Augmented

The augmented chord is also used as a passing chord, most commonly between any major chord and the minor chord a third below it. For example, some of The Beatles' early songs use this progression: D, D^{aug}, Bm. Chuck Berry also used this dissonant chord at the beginning of 'No Particular Place To Go' to represent a car-horn.

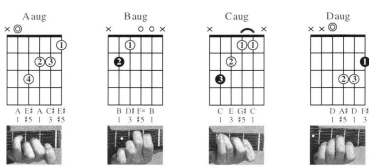

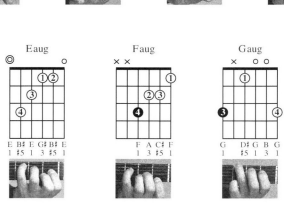

Variations on the dominant seventh chord are shown in these four chord boxes. The fifth note can be raised or lowered by a semitone for a different tone-colour. These 'altered seventh' chords are popular in jazz and 'cabaret' standards of the 30s, 40s and 50s.

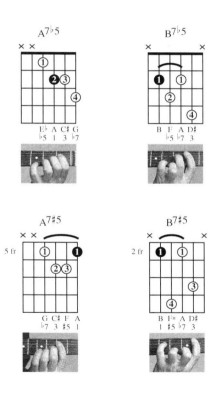

Suspended Fourth

After the sevenths, we come to the suspended chords. The suspended fourth is formed by removing ('suspending') the middle note of the chord and replacing it with the fourth of the scale. **Csus4 = C F G.**

This removal or suspension of the third (E) is very significant. Compare C major (C E G) with C minor (C E♭ G). The only difference is the note in the middle, the third. Take that away and how would you tell whether the chord was major or minor? For this reason, the suspended fourth is harmonically neutral - neither major nor minor - similar to a fifth, or power-chord.

The sus4 is a dramatic chord which is used to create tension and release, and to generally intensify the sound or emotion of a piece of music. The Who's 'Pinball Wizard' is one of the best examples of the suspended fourth in rock.

Here are seven suspended fourths.

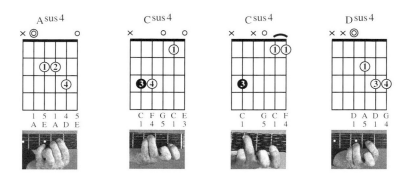

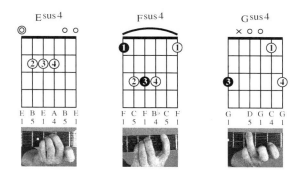

E sus 4
E B E A B E
1 5 1 4 5 1

F sus 4
F C F B♭ C F
1 5 1 4 5 1

G sus 4
G   D G C G
1   5 1 4 1

Moveable Shapes

Use the B sus 4 and the F♯ sus 4 moveable shapes to find any others you need.

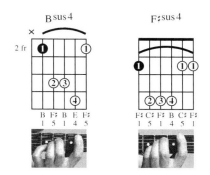

B sus 4
2 fr
B F♯ B E F♯
1 5 1 4 5

F♯ sus 4
F♯ C♯ F♯ B C♯ F♯
1 5 1 4 5 1

43

Dominant Seventh Suspended Fourth

This is a variant on the suspended fourth. The dominant seventh suspended fourth is made by suspending the third in a dominant seventh. C^{7sus4} = **C F G B♭**. It is also neither major nor minor.

Here are eight dominant 7 sus4 chord shapes. Use the B^{7sus4} and the F^{7sus4} as moveable shapes.

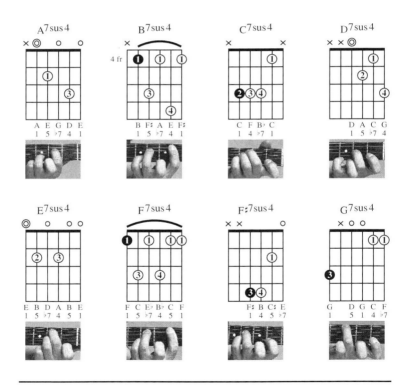

The suspended second is formed in a similar way to the suspended fourth - by removing the middle note of the chord. This time it's replaced with the second note of the scale. $C^{sus2} = C\ D\ G$. Likewise, the suspended second chord is neither major nor minor.

Here are seven suspended seconds. Use the B^{sus2} barre shape as a moveable chord - and find some more up the neck.

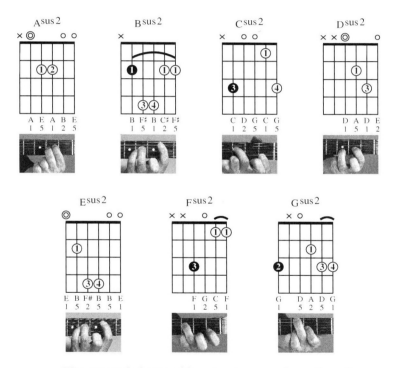

The suspended second is not as tense or dramatic as the suspended fourth. It has a slightly empty quality, making it good for slow, atmospheric ballads.

Dominant Seventh Suspended Second

This is a variant on the suspended second - and similar to the dominant 7 ^{sus4}, except that the third is replaced with the second, rather than the fourth note of the scale. C^{7sus2} = **C D G B$\flat$**. This chord should not be confused with C dominant ninth (C E G B$\flat$ D) where the third (E) is also present.

Here are seven chord shapes. Use the B^{7sus2} and the F^{7sus2} to find others up the neck.

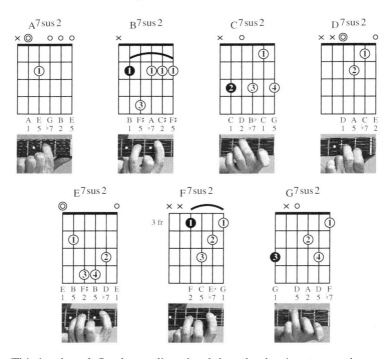

A^{7sus2}	B^{7sus2}	C^{7sus2}	D^{7sus2}
A E G B E	B F♯ A C♯ F♯	C D B♭ C G	D A C E
1 5 ♭7 2 5	1 5 ♭7 2 5	1 2 ♭7 1 5	1 5 ♭7 2

E^{7sus2}	F^{7sus2}	G^{7sus2}
E B F♯ B D E	F C E♭ G	G D A D F
1 5 2 5 ♭7 1	2 5 ♭7 1	1 5 2 5 ♭7

This is a less defined-sounding chord than the dominant seventh suspended fourth, having a vague, slightly dreamy sound. The presence of the second 'softens' the seventh.

Here is the major sixth chord - formed by adding the sixth note of the scale to a basic major triad. $C^6 = C E G A$.

Compare the shape C^{6*} in the last box with the barred C^6. You will often find C^{6*} in sheet music books - but this isn't actually a proper sixth because it doesn't have a G in it. It's essential to understand the difference, as if you take the fifth out of a sixth chord you end up with a first inversion minor! The C^{6*} is in fact Am/C.

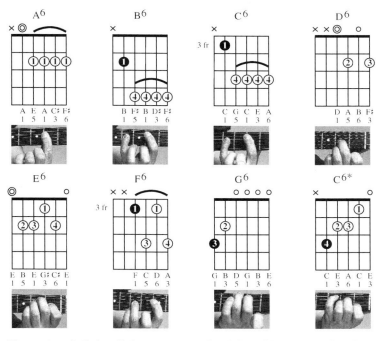

The major sixth is a light, summery chord found in pop, soul and jazz. The Beatles used sixths in their early songs, both on the guitar and in their vocal harmonising.

The minor flat sixth is created by adding the flattened sixth note of the major scale to the basic minor triad. $Cm^{\flat}6 = C\ E^{\flat}\ G\ A^{\flat}$. It is also harmonically close to the major seventh: if the notes are re-ordered we have $A^{\flat}\ C\ E^{\flat}\ G = A^{\flat}maj7$.

The chord has a strong minor feel and sounds really tense. Here are seven minor flat sixths.

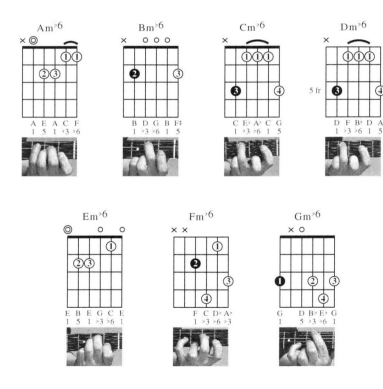

Minor Sixth

The minor sixth is created by adding the sixth note of the major scale to the minor triad. $Cm^6 = C\ E\flat\ G\ A$. Notice that if you take your finger off the D string in the Am^6 shape you create D^7.

The chord has a pungent, edgy quality, and is used where a haunting or tense atmosphere is required. You'll hear it in the James Bond Theme, and at the start of The Beatles' *Happiness Is A Warm Gun*.

Here are seven minor sixths.

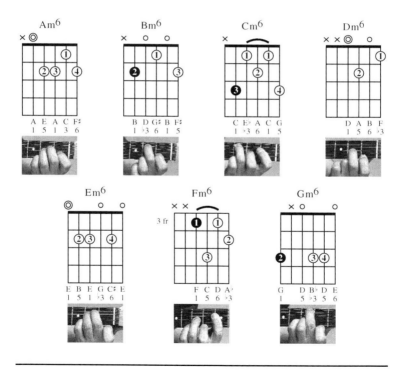

Dominant Seventh Sharp Ninth

Here is the dominant seventh sharp nine chord (or dom$^{7\#9}$). As you might have guessed, it is formed by simply sharpening the 9th note in the dominant ninth chord.

In C, this would be: **C E G B♭ D♯**. Below are four examples of this chord.

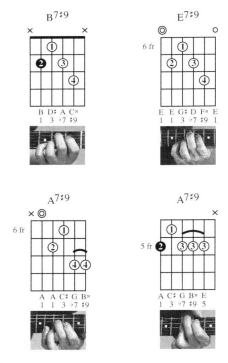

The dom$^{7\#9}$ is a rock favourite, which Jimi Hendrix made his own on songs like 'Purple Haze'. Of the four, boxes 2 and 4 are the moveable shapes.

All of the chords we've looked at so far fall within what can be termed the 'First Octave' - i.e: they can be entirely formed using the notes of just one octave.

The first of the 'Second Octave' chords are the ninths. These are formed by adding the ninth note of the scale to the dominant seventh chord. **C9 = C E G B♭ D**.

The dominant ninth is the most popular of the ninth chords, featuring in '50s rock'n'roll and '60s R'n'B. The ninth slightly softens the angularity of the dominant seventh.

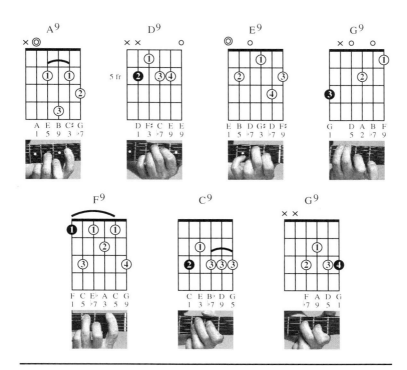

Major Ninth

This is formed by taking the major seventh chord and adding the ninth on top. In this instance the ninth dilutes some of the richness of the major seventh.

Once again, the third is still present. Compare C^{maj9} (C E G B D) with the C^{sus2} chord (C D G) on page 45. The difference should be clear!

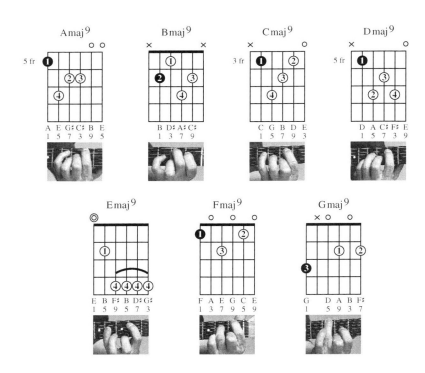

As with other chord types we've looked at, the addition of the seventh makes this considerably less intense compared to the minor add ninth (see page 55).

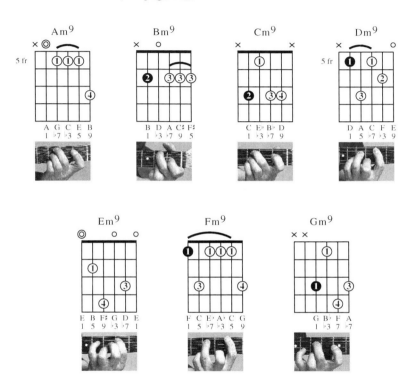

Ninth chords can also be found in altered forms if the fifth is flattened or sharpened. You can omit the fifth altogether sometimes in order to construct a playable shape.

Major Add Ninth

As its name suggests, this is a straight major chord with a ninth added. The difference between this and the dominant ninth is that the seventh note is not present.

For this reason this chord is sometimes confused with the sus2 chord. Here's a handy rule to remember: if a note is added from outside the original octave, the third is still present. In a sus chord, the third is *replaced* by the 2nd or 4th.

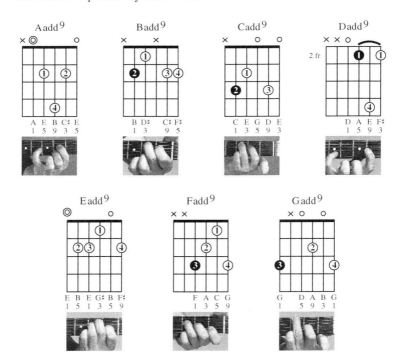

This chord is popular in pop and rock music, with the ninth adding interest to the straight major chord.

Obviously, 9th's can be added to minor chords too. In Cminor, the chord is simply **C E♭ G D** (the seventh is not present). Hear how, by simply adding the ninth, the chord becomes more expressive. The Bm add9 and Fm add9 are moveable shapes.

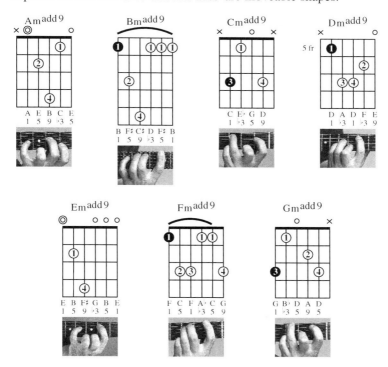

This is an extremely expressive chord in which the ninth actually intensifies the melancholy sound of the minor chord. It is good for haunting moments.

Making New Shapes - Major Chords

One of the great things about playing the guitar is experimenting and finding exciting new chords for yourself. One of the ways you can do this is to work with a shape you already know.

These ten chord boxes show what happens when you start with a barre chord of F (1) then take the barre off but keep the bass note (2). Notice that every time the shape is moved up it forms a different type of chord, not just the same type at a different pitch (as would be the case with a standard moveable shape).

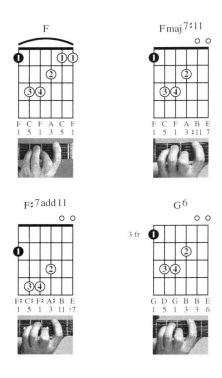

The reason lies with the open strings. The fretted notes retain their relationship to each other, a major chord (check the numbers 1, 3, 5). The open strings stay at the same pitch but change their harmonic relationship to the fretted notes.

A add 9

A	E	A	C♯	B	E
1	5	1	3	9	5

B add 11

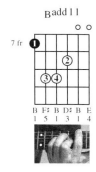

B	F♯	B	D♯	B	E
1	5	1	3	1	4

C maj 7

C	G	C	E	B	E
1	5	1	3	1	4

C♯ 7♯9

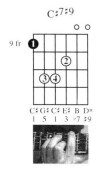

C♯	G♯	C♯	E♯	B	D×
1	5	1	3	♭7	♯9

D 6/9

D	A	D	F♯	B	E
1	5	1	3	6	9

E

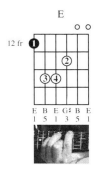

E	B	E	G♯	B	E
1	5	1	3	5	1

Making New Shapes - Minor Chords

You can do the same thing with a minor chord. F♯m becomes F♯m^{7}add^{11} when the barre is taken off. As the shape is moved up the neck some great new chords are formed with the top two strings ringing out. Try combining these with some of the previous major shapes.

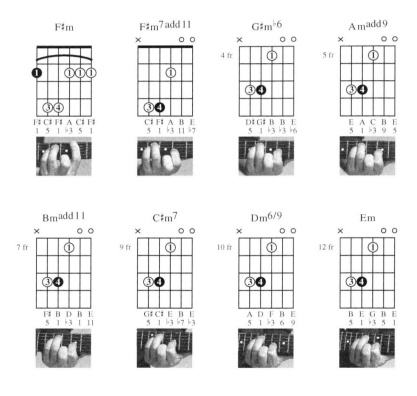

Here's a variation on the same approach. Take a D chord shape and simply move it up the fretboard. The fretted notes remain a major triad but the open string D relates to each shape in a slightly different way.

This moving D shape has often been used in folk songs. Listen to Led Zeppelin's 'Over The Hills And Far Away' to hear it in action!

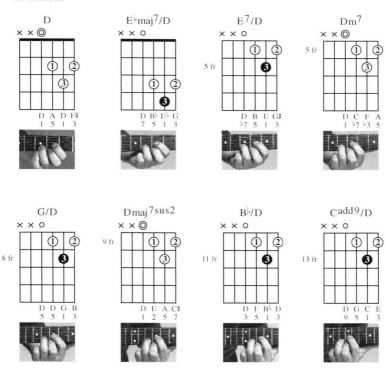

Top Three Triads

Here are six triads - three major, three minor - which you can move up and down the neck on the top three strings. Listen for the places where they sound better.

Major Triads

5 1 3

3 5 1

1 3 5

Minor Triads

1 ♭3 5

♭3 5 1

1 ♭3 5

Experiment with these shapes - try them in other places on the fretboard and see what you can find!

How Many Chord Types Are There?

In this Little Book Of Chords we've covered some of the most played chords and given you some ideas for finding more. One question people often ask is how many more chord types are there?

First, we looked at chords which fell within what can be termed the 'First Octave'. This means that if you take a scale - say C major, which is C D E F G A B C - they can be formed within this scale and without needing an extension of the scale into a second octave. Then we looked at chords from the 'Second Octave' group which included ninths and elevenths.

Elevenths and thirteenths are important in jazz but much less significant in pop and rock. They are complex chords, having no less than six or seven different notes. This means that a correct thirteenth is impossible to play on a six-string guitar. It also means that they are difficult to finger and 'voice'. When guitarists play elevenths and thirteenths they are often playing abbreviated versions of these chords in which some notes are necessarily missed out.

To finish, here is a quick look at thirty different chord types all based on the note G, which will give you an idea of the sheer variety of chord tones.

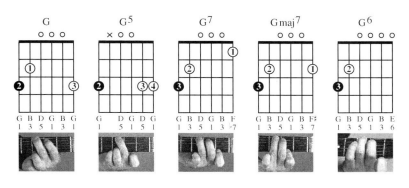

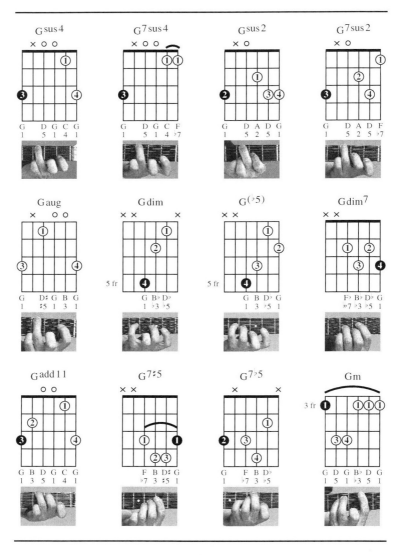

G sus 4

× ○ ○

G	D	G	C	G
1	5	1	4	1

G 7 sus 4

× ○ ○

G	D	G	C	F
1	5	1	4	♭7

G sus 2

× ○

G	D	A	D	G
1	5	2	5	1

G 7 sus 2

× ○

G	D	A	D	F
1	5	2	5	♭7

G aug

× ○ ○

G	D♯	G	B	G
1	♯5	1	3	1

G dim

× × ×

5 fr

G	B♭	D♭
1	♭3	♭5

G (♭5)

× ×

5 fr

G	B	D♭	G
1	3	♭5	1

G dim 7

× ×

F♯	B♭	D♭	G
♭♭7	♭3	♭5	1

G add 11

○ ○

G	B	D	G	C	G
1	3	5	1	4	1

G 7♯5

× ×

F	B	D♯	G
♭7	3	♯5	1

G 7♭5

×   ×

G	F	B	D♭
1	♭7	3	♭5

Gm

3 fr

G	D	G	B♭	D	G
1	5	1	♭3	5	1

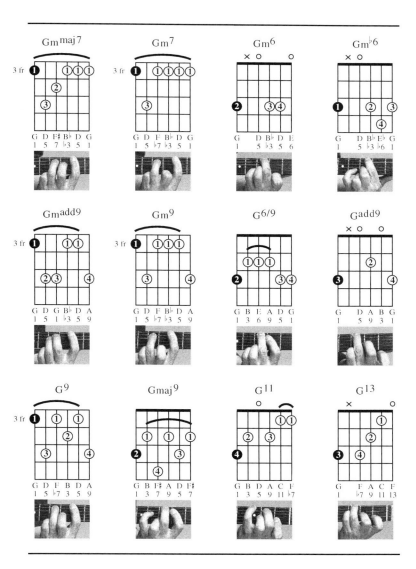

Gm maj7

3 fr

G D F# Bb D G
1 5 7 b3 5 1

Gm7

3 fr

G D F Bb D G
1 5 b7 b3 5 1

Gm6

× ○   ○

G   D Bb D E
1   5 b3 5 6

Gm b6

× ○

G   D Bb Eb G
1   5 b3 b6 1

Gmadd9

3 fr

G D G Bb D A
1 5 1 b3 5 9

Gm9

3 fr

G D F Bb D A
1 5 b7 b3 5 9

G6/9

G B E A D G
1 3 6 9 5 1

Gadd9

× ○   ○

G   D A B G
1   5 9 3 1

G9

3 fr

G D F B D A
1 5 b7 3 5 9

Gmaj9

G B F# A D F#
1 3 7 9 5 7

G11

○

G B D A C F
1 3 5 9 11 b7

G13

×   ○

G   F A C F
1   b7 9 11 13

63

Further Reading

Check out some of the other books in this new series, listed below. These, and many other great titles, are available from all good music retailers, or in case of difficulty, from the Music Sales catalogue, or click on our website: **musicsales.co.uk.**

The Little Book of Tips and Tricks (for Guitar)
AM954767

This book has everything you need to know to improve your guitar technique, instantly! Sections on equipment, playing rhythm, how to solo, and how to play like the pros!

The Little Book of Love Lyrics
AM954822

The lyrics to 35 of your favourite old and new love-songs, including 'Could It Be Magic', 'I Will Always Love You', 'Take My Breath Away' and 'Wonderful Tonight'.

The Little Book of Musical Terms
AM954866

A bite-size musical dictionary including definitions for both classical and contemporary music styles, notation and theory, instruments - from viol to modern electric guitar, and recording and music business terms. The perfect size for your music case!

The Little Book of Music Theory
AM954855

An introduction to Music Theory, including sections on accidentals, rhythm, major and minor keys, intervals, modes and chords. The perfect companion to The Little Book of Musical Terms!

Music Sales Limited Newmarket Road Bury St Edmunds Suffolk IP33 3YB
Tel: 01284 702 600